Original title:

Shadows in Snow

Author: Paulina Pähkel

ISBN HARDBACK: 978-9916-79-924-6

ISBN PAPERBACK: 978-9916-79-925-3

ISBN EBOOK: 978-9916-79-926-0

Frosty Shadows Cast in Twilight

As daylight fades to dusky gray,
Frosty shadows silently play.
Beneath the trees, where whispers sigh,
The chilly breeze breathes a goodbye.

Twinkling stars begin to gleam,
Light now dances like a dream.
Moonlight spills on icy streams,
Frosty shadows weave their themes.

Enshrouded Figures Beneath White Layers

In the stillness of the night,
Figures cloaked in purest white.
Softly caked in snowy beds,
Dreams afloat in frozen threads.

Whispers echo, softly bound,
Nature's silence all around.
Beneath the layers, secrets keep,
In the tranquility, we sleep.

Serpentine Steps on a Winter’s Path

Curving trails through drifting snow,
Winding whispers, soft and slow.
Footprints left in fleeting light,
Guide us through the frosty night.

Branches arch as shadows loom,
Winter's magic starts to bloom.
Every step, a tale retold,
Serpentine path, both young and old.

Muffled Calls Beneath the Blizzards

In the tempest, voices fade,
Muffled calls in snow's cascade.
Through the storm, the echoes lie,
Carried softly, near and nigh.

Lost in flurries, warmth feels far,
Yet we're guided by a star.
Under blizzards, hearts unite,
Muffled calls still bring the light.

The Lure of Hidden Tracks

In the forest deep, whispers call,
Footprints beckon, winter's thrall.
Each bend reveals a secret trace,
Nature's dance, a quiet embrace.

Snowflakes veil the world in white,
Shadows merge with fading light.
Paths forgotten, lost in time,
Adventure waits, a silent rhyme.

Beneath the canopy, tales unfold,
Of wanderers brave, of legends bold.
Every step tells stories anew,
In hidden tracks, dreams pursue.

From burbling brooks to soaring trees,
The call of nature stirs the breeze.
Chasing spirits, wandering far,
Guided softly by a star.

As twilight comes, the world sleeps deep,
In these tracks, sweet memories keep.
The lure of hidden paths endures,
Forever here, adventure lures.

Subtle Forms in the Winter Glow

Soft shadows dance in evening light,
Figures form, then fade from sight.
Glimmers trace the icy lakes,
Whispers echo, the stillness wakes.

Branches laden with snowy crowns,
Nature's artistry knows no bounds.
Each subtle form, a fleeting grace,
In the glow, time holds its place.

Frozen ponds mirror the sky,
Reflecting dreams that float on high.
Frosted edges, delicate dreams,
Life emerges in glistening streams.

Amidst the hush, the heart will see,
The warmth of winter's harmony.
Softly spoken in frosty air,
Love is found, everywhere.

Underneath the snowflakes' flight,
Lie the whispers of pure delight.
Subtle forms in twilight show,
Beauty thrives in the winter glow.

Dimmed Echoes of Frosted Paths

In the silence where shadows play,
Echoes linger at the end of day.
Frosted trails, a ghostly thread,
Where footsteps whisper, softly tread.

Through the mist, pale figures roam,
In winter's grasp, they find a home.
From muted hues spring tales long past,
In frozen moments, stories cast.

The crunch of snow beneath each step,
Memories held, each one adept.
Voices fade, yet still they sing,
Of joys and sorrows that winter brings.

Dimmed echoes rise, gently unfold,
Sunset's brush paints the world in gold.
Hidden paths yield treasures bright,
In the heart of the cold, pure light.

With every shadow, secrets thrive,
Frosted paths keep dreams alive.
In the quiet, let echoes flow,
Dimmed yet vivid, in moonlight's glow.

Specters Wrapped in a Blanket of White

Whispers of winter in silence weave,
Shadows of night, where dreams believe.
Wrapped in stillness, secrets hold tight,
Specters arise in the veil of white.

Moonlight glimmers on frost-kissed ground,
Echoes of laughter, no longer found.
A dance of ghosts in the softest glow,
Through the cold, their stories flow.

Gentle footprints in snowflakes trace,
Memories linger, a ghostly embrace.
Silent and soft, they drift away,
Lost in the magic of winter's play.

With every breath, a tale unfolds,
Frozen moments, warm hearts hold.
In the blanket of white, they softly sigh,
Specters of yore, as time drifts by.

Luminous Hues in the Cold

The dawn breaks softly, a canvas bright,
Luminous hues, chasing the night.
Shadows retreat in the morning's embrace,
Colors of hope in a frosty space.

Crimson and gold in the winter air,
Painted horizons, so vivid and rare.
Each brushstroke whispers to hearts once lost,
A tapestry woven, no matter the cost.

The chill in the breeze carries tales anew,
Of dreams reborn in the golden hue.
Silhouettes dancing on the icy lake,
A symphony played, in stillness they wake.

As sunlight kisses the frostbitten trees,
Nature's art whispers on the winter breeze.
In every shimmer, in every glow,
Luminous hues teach our hearts to grow.

Frostbitten Fables of the Night

In the heart of winter, tales are spun,
Fables of frost beneath the unseen sun.
Every whisper holds a story's might,
In the hush of the world, on this starry night.

Snowflakes whisper secrets soft and low,
Glimmers of truth in the moon's pale glow.
Winds carry fables from ages past,
Frozen in time, shadows cast.

Creatures of magic tread lightly here,
A dance of legends, drawing us near.
Frostbitten dreams weave through the air,
In the stillness of night, all whispers share.

The quiet holds mysteries, wrapped in frost,
Stories of what once was, never lost.
With every breath, the night does weave,
Frostbitten fables, we dare to believe.

Silent Footprints in the Frost

Silent footprints in the morning light,
Echoes of journeys, soft and slight.
Through the white blanket, paths intertwine,
Marking the passage of time, divine.

The frozen ground tells tales untold,
Of travelers' dreams in the bitter cold.
With each step taken, stories unfold,
In silence, the heart finds warmth to hold.

Beneath the canvas of snow so deep,
Frosty secrets in shadows creep.
Each imprint a memory, gentle and shy,
Singing of moments that whisper bye.

As dawn breaks gently, the world awakes,
Silent footprints, a trail that makes.
A testament of winter's gentle bid,
Tracks of the heart, where hopes are hid.

Pale Echoes of the Moonlit Glade

In the glade where shadows play,
Whispers stir the calm of night,
Moonlight spills in silver spray,
Dreams take wing, and hearts take flight.

Breezes carry secrets low,
Through the trees, they weave a song,
Guiding footsteps soft and slow,
In this place where souls belong.

Pale echoes of a timeless past,
Mingle with the stars above,
Moments fleeting, yet they last,
Wrapped in tender, silent love.

Nighttime blooms with fragrant grace,
Petals kissed by lunar beams,
In this sacred, hallowed space,
Nature wraps us in her dreams.

As dawn's light begins to creep,
Fading softly, night departs,
In the glade, the memories keep,
Pale echoes in our hearts.

Frosty Whispers of the Past

In the hush where echoes dwell,
Frosty whispers call the day,
Memories weave their secret spell,
In the cold, they gently sway.

Footprints left in icy dew,
Trace the paths of yesteryears,
Silent tales of me and you,
Bringing forth forgotten tears.

Beneath the trees, the shadows cling,
Breath of winter paints the scene,
In the stillness, all is spring,
In the heart of the evergreen.

Raindrops kissed by frosty air,
Dancing on the edge of fate,
Whispers linger everywhere,
Time awaits, it cannot wait.

Frosty winds, they softly blow,
Carrying the dreams we had,
In this chill, our spirits grow,
Bound by joy, both sweet and sad.

Luminescent Formations in the Chill

In the night, the stars align,
Luminescent forms appear,
Carved by frost, a bright design,
Whispering what we hold dear.

Ice and light in harmony,
Beneath the moon’s soft embrace,
Nature's art, a tapestry,
Crafted with a gentle grace.

Snowflakes dance in silver flight,
Sparkling like a million dreams,
In this spell of wintry night,
Magic flows in crystal streams.

Upon the earth, a canvas white,
Each formation tells a tale,
Guided by the soft moonlight,
Nights like these, we cannot fail.

Through the chill, our hearts ignite,
Finding warmth in what is still,
Luminescence in the night,
Breathless beauty, time will thrill.

Moonlit Traces on Silver Fields

On the fields of silvery glow,
Moonlit traces guide our way,
Footsteps soft, as gently flow,
Carried on the breath of day.

In the stillness, shadows dance,
Casting dreams in quiet grace,
Every moment holds a chance,
To explore this sacred space.

With each step, a story grows,
Woven in the night's embrace,
Beneath the moon, our journey flows,
Time forgotten, we find place.

Stars alight, the night awakes,
Lighting paths we dare to roam,
In this land, our spirit shakes,
Every heart can find a home.

As dawn breaks, the vision fades,
But the moonlight will remain,
In our hearts, the memory wades,
Tracing paths through joy and pain.

The Dance of Frosted Shapes

In mornings soft, the frost awakes,
Gentle whispers, nature shakes.
Crystals twirl on winter's stage,
A ballet pure, the world engaged.

Moonlight drapes on silent streams,
As shadows play in crystal beams.
Amongst the pines, the chill does creep,
While winter's dreams invade our sleep.

Each flake descends, a fleeting star,
Creating wonders near and far.
With grace they dance, a lonesome flight,
In icy gowns, they're draped in white.

The air is still, the night serene,
Painted landscapes, pure and clean.
Nature's art in frozen time,
A silent song, a whispered rhyme.

So let us pause, take in the view,
Embrace the cold, the world anew.
For in this dance of frosted shapes,
The heart finds warmth, the spirit escapes.

Enigmas Amidst the Winter White

Veiled in layers, secrets lie,
Snowflakes falling from the sky.
Softly whispered, tales unfold,
Enigmas in the winter's cold.

Footprints lead to places unknown,
Paths erased, the stories sown.
Beneath the surface, beauty sprawls,
In winter's grasp, the silence calls.

Crisp air dances with a sigh,
Nature breathes, and wonders fly.
Frosted limbs and muted sounds,
A canvas white, where magic bounds.

Through swirling winds, the mysteries sing,
Of transient life, the joys they bring.
Each fallen leaf, a vessel of tales,
In winter's grip, all tracks and trails.

So pause awhile, let thoughts take flight,
In the embrace of winter white.
The enigmas linger, softly bright,
In the silence of the snowy night.

Shadows of Silence on Winter’s Breath

In the twilight, shadows loom,
Winter's breath, a silent boom.
Crisp the air, a soft caress,
In stillness wrapped, the world does rest.

Branches bare, against the grey,
Whispers float, then drift away.
Every flake, a secret cast,
On winter's path, the die is fast.

Shades of twilight, wrapped in glow,
Gentle echoes, low and slow.
Crimson hues beneath the frost,
In silence kept, what’s gained, what's lost?

Patterns weave in the moonlight's beam,
The spirit stirs, a vibrant dream.
Through frozen fields, a hush persists,
In winter's spell, the heart insists.

So let the night embrace the chill,
Feel the quiet, embrace the thrill.
For in the shadows, life is penned,
In winter's silence, we ascend.

Condensed Dreams in the Chill

Beneath the frost, dreams softly lie,
In a world where echoes sigh.
Each breath that forms a misty cloud,
Whispers stories, whispers loud.

As the chill grips, the heart can feel,
Frozen thoughts that softly reel.
In silent nights, visions bright,
Condensed dreams in silver light.

Falling stars through winter's veil,
Guide the heart along the trail.
With hopeful glimmers, shadows blend,
In the chill, the heart can mend.

Every flake an unspoken thought,
In the stillness, lessons taught.
Embrace the quiet, let it spill,
Keep your dreams against the chill.

So paint your dreams in frosty hue,
Let every wish be born anew.
In the cold, find warmth's embrace,
Condensed dreams in winter’s space.

Shades of Winter’s Breath

Whispers of frost dance in the air,
Silent shadows drape everywhere.
Icicles hang like fragile glass,
Time stands still, moments pass.

Trees wear coats of shimmering white,
Nature's wonder, pure delight.
Footprints trace a hidden path,
In winter's quiet, we find its math.

The world is hushed in gentle calm,
Snowflakes drift, soft as a psalm.
Each breath creates a misty plume,
A fleeting echo in the gloom.

Beneath the cover, life sleeps tight,
Dreaming of warmth, of radiant light.
Yet in the stillness, seeds are sown,
Winter's breath, a whispered tone.

As shadows deepen, stars burst bright,
Guiding us through the frosty night.
In the heart of winter, beauty lies,
In every breath, the world complies.

The Dance of Ice and Light

In the morning's light, crystals glow,
Painting the world in a delicate show.
The ice swirls softly in the breeze,
Each sparkle dances with graceful ease.

Sunbeams kiss the frozen ponds,
Life awakens in whispered songs.
Reflecting skies in silver hue,
Nature's palette, ever anew.

Branches tremble, laden with frost,
In this moment, nothing is lost.
A symphony of chill and cheer,
Echoes of winter, crystal clear.

We twirl amid the glistening white,
As day fades softly into night.
Each breath a note in winter's tune,
Under the watchful eye of the moon.

A ballet of shadows, soft and bright,
The dance continues, a pure delight.
In every flake, a story's spun,
In the heart of winter, we become one.

Secrets Beneath the Frozen Surface

Beneath the ice, secrets dwell,
In a world where stories swell.
Silent tales in frozen depths,
Life hidden, holding its breaths.

The whisper of currents, soft and low,
Where unseen wonders start to grow.
A sanctuary, crisp and clear,
Holding memories, year by year.

Each crack in the ice tells a tale,
Of seasons past, of sun and hail.
Frozen echoes, a soft refrain,
Beneath the surface, nothing is plain.

In hidden chambers, life abides,
Amidst the frost, where nature hides.
A world suspended, calm and deep,
In winter's grasp, the secrets sleep.

As spring nears, the thaw begins,
Revealing truths where life wins.
What lies beneath, we can't ignore,
In the thawing, we find so much more.

Celestial Prints on a Blank Canvas

The sky unfurls, a canvas bare,
Stars emerge in quiet flair.
Swirling lights in velvet night,
Each twinkle holds a dream in sight.

The moon, a brush dipped in gleam,
Letters whispered in the dream.
Galaxies twirl in cosmic dance,
Inviting hearts to take a chance.

With every stroke, the night unfolds,
Stories of love, of daring souls.
In the stillness, thoughts collide,
In celestial prints, we take pride.

A tapestry of dark and bright,
Guiding us through the tranquil night.
As cosmic winds weave through the air,
We find our peace, we find our care.

Infinite wonders above us wait,
Each star an echo of fate.
In the expanse where dreams take flight,
Celestial prints, our hearts ignite.

Echoes of the Forgotten Path

Whispers linger through the trees,
Steps unmade on paths of dreams.
Shadows dance beneath the ferns,
Where the earth in silence yearns.

A story woven in the mist,
Fragments of a dawn once kissed.
Time's embrace holds tight to fate,
In echoes soft, we contemplate.

Footfalls trace a wanderer's tale,
Through the woods where voices pale.
Lost in thought, the heart confides,
A journey where the spirit glides.

In every bend, a memory gleams,
Fleeting, like the sun's warm beams.
Forgotten paths still call our way,
Through tangled roots of yesterday.

Even as the light departs,
The path remains within our hearts.
In twilight's glow, we seek what's true,
The forgotten path leads back to you.

Twilight’s Ghosts in Winter’s Realm

Beneath the frost, the whispers creep,
Where shadows blend, and silence sleeps.
Ghosts of twilight linger near,
Echoing secrets we hold dear.

In the chill of winter's breath,
Time stands still, eluding death.
Midst flurries white, our visions fade,
As twilight’s ghosts begin their trade.

Softly the evening's colors blend,
In shimmering light, the shadows mend.
A dance remembered, pasts collide,
In winter's grip our hearts abide.

Barren branches reach for skies,
Adrift in dreams, the spirit flies.
In the hush, the world unfolds,
Twilight's ghosts in winter's hold.

The moonlight whispers through the trees,
As echoes float on winter's breeze.
In this realm where silence thrives,
Twilight’s ghosts keep hope alive.

Lurking Memories Beneath the Snow

Underneath the cold, white veil,
Memories whisper, soft and frail.
Frozen echoes sing of days,
When laughter danced in golden rays.

Beneath the snow, the stories lie,
Silent dreams that once could fly.
Shadows linger, soft and wraith,
Guarding tales of love and faith.

Frosty nights hold secrets dear,
In every flake, a dream appears.
Buried deep, yet ever clear,
Lurking memories, always near.

In quiet woods, the heart reflects,
On paths unseen, the time connects.
Each fallen flake a muse's sigh,
In timeless dance, beneath the sky.

Awakened by the spring's sweet song,
The memories return, where they belong.
Beneath the snow, the heart will know,
What once was lost, begins to grow.

Frost-Kissed Secrets of the Night

In moonlit hues, the frost descends,
A tranquil night as daylight bends.
Whispers float on chilly air,
Wrapped in dreams, beyond compare.

Secrets gleam on silvered ground,
Voices of the night resound.
Every shadow holds a tale,
In the quiet, we prevail.

Stars above, like watchers keen,
Illuminate the sights unseen.
Within the dark, our hearts conspire,
Frost-kissed secrets, pure desire.

Winds caress the frozen land,
Weaving threads with gentle hands.
In the silence, love ignites,
Frost-kissed secrets of the night.

Through the frost, the world emerges,
Softly sang by nature's urges.
In the stillness, spirits play,
Frost-kissed dreams will lead the way.

Whispers Beneath the Snowfall

Soft whispers float through the air,
Snowflakes dance without a care.
Trees wear blankets, white and bright,
Silence reigns, a peaceful night.

Footsteps crunch on frozen ground,
In this stillness, magic's found.
Nature's breath is crisp and clear,
Warming hearts that gather near.

In each flake, a story told,
Of winter's charm, both brave and bold.
Stars twinkle in the abyss,
A subtle promise, winter's kiss.

Time slows down beneath the glow,
Of frosty realms, where soft winds blow.
Hold this moment, cherish it tight,
In whispers soft, the stars ignite.

As dawn breaks, soft colors rise,
Painting dreams across the skies.
Winter's song begins to flow,
In echoes sweet, beneath the snow.

Echoes of Winter's Veil

Echoes linger in the night,
Winter's breath, a ghostly sight.
Through the trees, the shadows dance,
In frosty air, we take a chance.

Moonlight bathes the frozen ground,
Every heartbeat, a distant sound.
Silvery mists wrap around,
Whispers of dreams yet unbound.

Branches bow with heavy weight,
Nature's pause, a longing state.
In this hush, we find our way,
Through starry paths, where spirits play.

Fires crackle, warmth is near,
In the cold, we draw you near.
Voices blend in harmony,
In winter's song, we'll always be.

As shadows fade, the night departs,
With every dawn, we share our hearts.
Echoes dwell where we have been,
In winter's veil, our souls begin.

Dark Traces on a White Canvas

Dark traces mark the purest snow,
Silent whispers start to flow.
Footprints lead where few have tread,
Unspeakable tales of the dead.

Each shadow holds a secret tight,
Underneath the cold moonlight.
Stories etched in stark contrast,
Fleeting moments, shadows cast.

Trees stand guard, a silent host,
Witnessing what we fear the most.
In the stillness, echoes ring,
Of all the loss that winter brings.

Yet in the dark, a spark can be,
Life that flows like a symphony.
Amidst the sorrow and the pain,
Beauty lingers like gentle rain.

So trace your path, embrace the night,
Hold close the dreams that feel so bright.
For as the snow begins to melt,
New stories wait, yet to be felt.

Secrets of the Icy Twilight

In twilight's grip, the world stands still,
Frozen whispers, time to kill.
A hidden realm where shadows play,
Secrets linger, dusk turns gray.

Crimson skies, the sun retreats,
Underneath the snow, heartbeats.
Glowing embers fade away,
As night encroaches, soft and gray.

Dreams are caught in icy webs,
Twilight's magic binds the ebbs.
Frosty gleams on barren trees,
A haunting tune on crisp, cold breeze.

Lose yourself in winter's sigh,
Where forgotten loves, like echoes, lie.
In silence, find the truths you seek,
As stars awake while shadows speak.

Secrets lie in every snowflake,
Tales of joy and joy's heartache.
Embrace the night, let go the past,
For in the twilight, dreams are cast.

Hidden Stories Under the Snow

Beneath the white, tales lie in wait,
Silent secrets, softly sedate.
Footsteps erased by winter's embrace,
Memories hidden in a cold, still place.

Frozen whispers drift through the air,
Echoes of laughter, moments to share.
Branches bow low, heavy with dreams,
Draped in a blanket, it softly gleams.

Nature's quilt wraps the world in peace,
Frosted breath, a moment's release.
Each flake a story, gently unfolds,
A tapestry woven with glimmers of gold.

Yet as the thaw brings warmth and light,
Ancient stories will take to flight.
Awakening dreams from their slumbered rest,\nRevealing
the beauty that winter has blessed.

In the melt, beneath the sun's glow,
Hidden stories start to flow.
Life blooms anew, but the snow will remain,
A reminder of tales etched in the grain.

Fragments of Nightfall in Ice

Stars ignite in the velvet night,
Frozen shards catch the pale moonlight.
Each glimmer a fragment, a fleeting glance,
A dance of shadows, a silent romance.

Whispers of dreams weave through the chill,
Echoes of hopes that linger still.
Crystals shimmer on the winter's breath,
Bearing the weight of stories of death.

The night holds secrets within its fold,
Fractured reflections, tales unfold.
The roar of silence, a stunning delight,
Fragments of nightfall, lost in the white.

Softly they tumble, a cascade of time,
Eternal moments, they rhythm and rhyme.
In the quiet of darkness, the ice does sing,
A ballad of what the cold nights bring.

In the dawn, as warmth starts to glow,
Silent reflections begin to flow.
Fragments dissolve in the light of day,
But the night will keep its magic at bay.

Stilled Whispers on Frozen Winds

Whispers drift softly on the cold breeze,
Carried away with the shivering trees.
Held in the frosty breath of the night,
Murmurs of stories hidden from sight.

Every gust tells of where it has been,
Fleeting memories caught in the thin.
Echoes of laughter, secrets so dear,
Trapped in the stillness, muted yet near.

Frozen winds cradle the tales of the past,
Layers of stillness, too fragile to last.
Frost on the branches, a silvery lace,
The chill in the air, a tender embrace.

As night deepens, the whispers entwine,
Every rustle, a reminder divine.
Voices of winter, soft and sincere,
Gathered for those who will pause to hear.

Though silence reigns in the heart of the cold,
Stilled whispers remain, vibrant and bold.
Lost in the swirling, they seek to be found,
In frozen winds, their truths resound.

Twilight Impressions in a Snowy World

As day gently fades to twilight's grace,
Snow blankets the earth in a soft embrace.
Colors dissolve in the dusky blue,
Impressions of warmth in the winter's view.

A hush falls over the still, white expanse,
Echoes of life in a frozen dance.
Each flake a brushstroke, art in the night,
A canvas of dreams, shimmering bright.

Shadows grow long as the stars appear,
Each twinkle holds a memory dear.
Twilight whispers of what lies ahead,
In the snowy world, where new paths are led.

The twilight lingers, time seems to pause,
In winter's hold, there's a gentle cause.
A moment of magic, sublime and profound,
In impressions of twilight, we're blissfully bound.

So let us wander through this snowy land,
With twilight's embrace by nature's hand.
In every step, let our hearts find their way,
Through a world of wonder, come what may.

Veiled Figures in the Sparkling Night

In twilight's glow, shadows creep,
Figures dance where secrets sleep.
Whispers float on cool night air,
Veiled in mystery, lost in care.

Stars above, they twinkle bright,
Casting dreams in the velvet night.
Veils of fog, they softly sway,
Guiding spirits on their way.

Moonlit paths that beckon near,
Echoes of laughter, soft and clear.
Fleeting forms both strange and wise,
In the darkness, magic lies.

Lost in thoughts of what might be,
A world unseen, a silent plea.
Through the mist, they glide and weave,
In the night, we dare believe.

Mysteries Hidden Beneath Soft Covers

Beneath the quilts, the stories thrive,
Softly tucked, they come alive.
Whispers linger, secrets swirl,
In this cocoon, the dreams unfurl.

Pages yellowed, tales unfold,
In their depths, the past retold.
Under cover, shadows play,
Lost in worlds, we drift away.

Soft the touch of fabric worn,
Wrapped in warmth, our hearts reborn.
In hushed tones, the night confides,
Mysteries where hope resides.

Fingers trace the lines of fate,
Every whisper, a silent weight.
Stories glisten, waiting there,
In the quiet, we declare.

Shrouded Glimmers of the Frigid Stars

In the stillness, stars enshroud,
Glimmers bright amidst the cloud.
Whispers of frost, cold and clear,
Calling to those who dare to hear.

Wrapped in shadows, night descends,
Hopes and dreams, the cosmos sends.
Crystalline wishes float above,
Shrouded light, the night we love.

Veils of ice upon the ground,
Silent echoes, a soft sound.
Shivering light, a graceful arc,
Guides the wanderer in the dark.

Frigid breath in winter's chill,
Stars that shine with frozen thrill.
Each flicker holds a story told,
In the sky so vast and bold.

Dreamlike Forms in the Winter Snow

In winter's hush, the world transforms,
Silent whispers, dreamlike forms.
Blankets white, they softly lay,
Cradling night, concealing day.

Footsteps muffled, secrets tread,
Through the drifts where spirits led.
Frozen figures, soft as grace,
In the snow, a quiet place.

Frosty breath hangs in the air,
Chilling thoughts, yet hearts laid bare.
In each flake, a story spun,
Dreams awaken one by one.

Veils of winter, magic bright,
Guiding dreams in soft twilight.
Through the frost, we come alive,
In the snow, our hopes survive.

Lingering Echoes of a Chilly Night

The stars whisper secrets, soft and bright,
Amid the shadows of a frosty night.
Moonlight dances, silver and bold,
Casting stories of warmth in the cold.

Footsteps crunch on the frozen ground,
Each echo a memory, profound.
Breezes carry tales from afar,
In the stillness, dreams are ajar.

Whispers of laughter, fading away,
As night departs, bringing the day.
Yet in the silence, time has its say,
Lingering echoes of yesterday.

Celestial Forms in a Winter’s Dream

Under the sky, in twilight's embrace,
Snowflakes waltz with effortless grace.
Stars above, twinkle with cheer,
In this canvas, all feels clear.

Frosty patterns on a windowpane,
Nature’s artistry, a beautiful stain.
The chill of night, a calming balm,
Wrapped in silence, the world is calm.

As dreams unfold, we drift and soar,
Through realms unseen, we explore.
Celestial wonders, vast and wide,
In winter’s embrace, we take a ride.

Silvery Etchings on Wood and Snow

Beneath the trees, the snowflakes fall,
Covering the whispers of nature's call.
Traces of life, etched in white,
Stories hidden from the night.

Each branch adorned in crystals bright,
Nature's diamonds catching light.
Footprints dance, a tale to tell,
In this silence, we fare well.

Softly the wind carries dreams away,
In the frosty air, they gently sway.
Silvery etchings tell a story,
Of fleeting moments, fleeting glory.

An Enigma Wrapped in White

A shroud of snow conceals the ground,
In whispers of silence, mysteries abound.
Nature holds secrets, locked away tight,
An enigma wrapped in the cloak of night.

Beneath the surface, life still thrives,
Hidden wonders, where magic derives.
Winter's grasp, both fierce and fair,
Breathes life anew in the chilly air.

Each flake a puzzle, scattered and small,
Yet together they form a wondrous thrall.
An enigma unfolds, under the moon,
In the heart of winter, we find our tune.

Whispers of the Cold Night

In silence wrapped, the stars do gleam,
A frosty breath, or so it seems.
The moonlight dances on the snow,
As shadows whisper soft and low.

Beneath the pine, a secret lies,
Where frost conceals the night's surprise.
The world is hushed, a quiet sight,
Embraced within the cold of night.

Each branch adorned with icy lace,
Reflects the stillness of this place.
The winds carry tales from afar,
Beneath the watchful, gleaming star.

A chill pervades the tranquil air,
With every step, a whispered prayer.
The night unfolds its mysteries,
In frozen dreams, the heart finds ease.

So listen close, for nature calls,
In every sound the spirit falls.
The cold night holds its ancient rites,
In whispered tones of wondrous sights.

Trails of Remnants Underneath

Beneath the snow, where secrets sleep,
Lie remnants of the past we keep.
Footprints marked from ages gone,
In silence, they weave tales upon.

The earth still breathes its memories,
In frozen ground, the history frees.
Each trail a story, faded, yet bold,
In quiet whispers, truths unfold.

Through drifting snow, the shadows play,
As ghosts of time just drift away.
The tales of old entwined with fate,
In every path we contemplate.

The season's touch, a fleeting hand,
Erases signs across the land.
Yet underneath the layers deep,
The heart of history will not sleep.

So journey forth, with eyes anew,
For every layer holds a clue.
The remnants tell the tales we seek,
In trails of time, the lost still speak.

Echoes of a Frozen Past

Echoes linger in the frost,
Memories of what was lost.
In the stillness, time stands still,
As shadows dance upon the hill.

A whisper floats on icy air,
Of tales entwined with cold despair.
The past is cloaked in crystal sheen,
A frozen place, a haunting scene.

In every flake, a story spun,
Of battles fought and races run.
The echoes call from times before,
Through fields of snow, we hear them roar.

With every breath, the past is near,
A ghostly hymn that we can hear.
In silence, echoes softly play,
A haunting tune of yesterday.

So heed the calls that time has cast,
In echoes, find the shadows cast.
The frozen past, a tale to tell,
In whispers deep, we know it well.

Shrouded Secrets of the Snowfield

In snowfield vast, secrets lie,
Beneath the drifts, the whispers sigh.
The world outside feels far away,
In silent magic, dreams at bay.

Each flake that falls holds tales untold,
Of warmth in winter, memories bold.
The chill that grips the heart so tight,
Conceals the secrets of the night.

A crystal maze, the path unknown,
Where quiet thoughts in silence grown.
The snow wraps all in pure embrace,
Hiding the past with gentle grace.

With every step, the stories awake,
From hidden depths, the echoes break.
In shrouded veils of white and grey,
The snowfield holds the night at bay.

So wander forth, through drifting snow,
For hidden truths, the heart must know.
In every flake, a secret sleeps,
In winter's arms, the silence keeps.

Mysterious Prints in the Winter Glow

In the hush of snow, silent trails,
Footprints whisper tales of gales.
Beneath the soft, pale winter light,
A dance of shadows fades from sight.

Frosted lace on sparkling ground,
Each imprint speaks, not a sound.
Wanderers lost in fleeting dreams,
Chasing echoes of silver beams.

Muffled steps in the evening chill,
Tracing paths on the icy hill.
What secrets lie just out of view?
A world concealed in shades of blue.

Wind carries sighs of ancient lore,
As darkness drapes forevermore.
In the quiet, spirits roam,
Leaving prints that guide us home.

Snowflakes fall, a gentle sigh,
Beneath the cold, the warmth will lie.
In each step, a story blooms,
Mysterious prints break through the glooms.

Ethereal Forms at Twilight's Edge

At twilight's gate, the shadows play,
Whispers linger, then drift away.
Shapes like dreams begin to blend,
Ethereal forms that twist and bend.

Faint silhouettes in the dusky light,
Dancing softly, just out of sight.
With each breath, the night unfolds,
Mysteries wrapped in silken folds.

Colors bleed in the fading day,
As visions swirl in a grand ballet.
In twilight's grasp, time lingers near,
An echo of laughter only we hear.

The horizon glows with a gentle hue,
Embracing all, both old and new.
Here in the dusk, we feel alive,
As forgotten whispers start to thrive.

Moonlight spills like liquid gold,
In these moments, life feels bold.
Ethereal forms, no need to flee,
For twilight's edge, a mystery.

Lattice of Frosted Footfalls

In the morning's chill, a web is spun,
Frosty patterns where we run.
Each footfall etches nature's art,
A lattice formed, a brand-new start.

With each step, the silence sings,
A beauty that the cold wind brings.
Glistening in the dawn's embrace,
Footprints weave a delicate lace.

Sculpted shapes in a world so white,
Frosted images of pure delight.
Transitory paths in the winter cold,
Stories of journeys silently told.

Nature's breath makes the canvas bright,
As dancers tread with soft, light might.
In this realm of icy grace,
Each frozen tread finds its place.

As the sun climbs, they slowly fade,
Whispers of journeys that time had made.
In the lattice of footprints, we see,
The fleeting beauty, wild and free.

Dappled Light on a Bleak Horizon

In the twilight, where colors blend,
Dappled light begins to tend.
Over hills, the shadows stretch,
A canvas where dreams are etched.

Bleak horizons embrace the dark,
Yet in the gloom, a hopeful spark.
Sunset bleeds into the night,
Casting whispers, soft and light.

Clouds drift lazily, a muted hue,
Painting the sky in shades of blue.
Each moment savory, sharp, and clear,
As day and night begin to near.

The world stands still, caught in the glow,
Dappled light on the ground below.
In the quiet, a promise lies,
For those who dare to seek the skies.

So let your heart embrace the change,
For in the dark, we are not estranged.
Dappled light, a fleeting grace,
Illuminates life's endless chase.

Veils of Mystery in the Winter Light

In the hush of winter's breath,
Shadows dance beneath the trees.
Frosty whispers weave a path,
Nature's secrets on the breeze.

Blankets white cover the ground,
Silent dreams in crystal hue.
Every flake a story bound,
Holding tales of skies so blue.

The sun peeks through veils so thin,
Glistening on the frozen lake.
Time seems still, the world begins,
To shimmer in the light we make.

Footsteps crunch in silence deep,
Echoes linger, soft and light.
In this wonder, souls can leap,
Finding peace in winter's night.

Each moment holds a breath of time,
As twilight falls, the stars ignite.
In the stillness, we find rhyme,
In veils of mystery, pure delight.

Intricate Designs of Icy Silence

Whispers swirl in frosty air,
Patterns form on window panes.
Nature's art, both rare and fair,
Glimmers caught in icy chains.

Crystals bloom like flowers bright,
A silent world, a soft embrace.
Every corner, every sight,
Greeted by the snow's sweet grace.

Gentle winds create a song,
Filling hearts with quiet peace.
Where the frozen moments throng,
All our worries seem to cease.

Snowflakes fall, a crafted dance,
Landing softly on the ground.
Each one carries a fix'd chance,
Of a story yet unbound.

In the stillness, time concedes,
To the art of winter's hand.
Life emerges from icy seeds,
Intricate designs so grand.

The Gray Ghosts of Winter's Breath

Fog rolls in like whispered tales,
Shrouding all in muted gray.
In the chill, a spirit wails,
Of the light that slipped away.

Trees stand bare, their branches stark,
Ghostly figures in the mist.
Every shadow leaves a mark,
Of the moments we have missed.

Footprints vanish, lost in time,
Echoes of the past remain.
In the winter's silent rhyme,
Haunting memories leave a stain.

A flicker here, a shimmer there,
Glimpses of what used to be.
In the stillness, we beware,
Of the stories yet to see.

As the daylight starts to creep,
Ghosts retreat into the light.
In the quiet, dreams can seep,
Winter's breath brings new insight.

Ephemeral Visions on a White Sheet

Blanket soft, the world anew,
Whispers held in snowy folds.
Every flake tells tales so true,
Of fleeting moments, dreams untold.

A canvas pure, untouched by time,
Imprinted thoughts in silence laid.
As footprints mark a crisp design,
Life unwinds, a fleeting braid.

Sunlight glints on wintry white,
Casting shadows, soft and long.
In the still, we find our light,
Harmonic echoes in a song.

Dreams take flight in the cold air,
On this sheet where visions gleam.
Each breath a thought, light as a prayer,
Painting life in a quiet dream.

As twilight draws the day to close,
The white sheet whispers to the night.
In this moment, beauty grows,
Ephemeral visions, pure delight.

Reflections of a Dusky Dream

In twilight's grace, shadows play,
Whispers of hope drift away,
Each breath a story, soft and deep,
Lost in the twilight, where dreams sleep.

Mirrors of thought in silent streams,
Echo the fabric of fragile dreams,
With every sigh, a flickering flame,
Illuminates paths, yet calls no name.

Beneath the hues of evening mist,
Every secret gently kissed,
Time dances lightly, a fleeting chance,
In dusk's embrace, we find our trance.

Stars awake to greet the night,
Guiding us with their distant light,
In every twinkle, a promise gleams,
Unlocking the doors of our hidden dreams.

As dawn approaches, dreams take flight,
Transforming shadows into light,
With every heartbeat, we will sing,
Reflections of life that twilight brings.

Unveiling Figures of the Frozen Night

In icy realms where silence dwells,
Figures dance like delicate spells,
Veils of frost on moonlit ground,
Whispers of secrets, softly found.

The crisp air bites, a tender sting,
Echoes of night begin to ring,
Stars adorn the celestial dome,
In this stillness, we wander home.

Shapes emerge in shadows cast,
Against the cold, the die is cast,
With every heartbeat, tales untold,
Unveiling wonders, brilliant and bold.

Veils of night wrap tight around,
Mysteries lost yet to be found,
Crystals shimmer, reflecting light,
In the embrace of the frozen night.

Beneath the cloak of winter’s breath,
Life whispers softly, defying death,
Every heartbeat, a silent vow,
To treasure the figures of night somehow.

Imprints of a Starlit Silence

Under the gaze of a starlit sky,
Echoes linger, a gentle sigh,
Imprints left on the velvet night,
Guiding souls with their soft light.

Whispers float in the cosmic sea,
Carving paths where hearts roam free,
In every sparkle, a moment shared,
In starlit silence, we are bared.

The fabric of night, woven tight,
Holds the dreams that take to flight,
With every twinkle, memories flash,
In this serene, celestial bash.

Barefoot on grass, we feel the glow,
In the tapestry of night, we flow,
Hand in hand, as we drift and sway,
Chasing the shadows that fade away.

As dawn beckons, we hold the peace,
In starlit silence, our hearts release,
A promise shines in the morning light,
That love endures beyond the night.

Crystalline Echoes of a Cold, Dark World

In the shadows of a frozen realm,
Crystalline echoes softly overwhelm,
Each breath we take, a frost-kissed air,
In darkened whispers, beauty laid bare.

The stillness hums with ancient songs,
Where time meanders, righting the wrongs,
With glimmers of light on frosted ground,
A tapestry of quiet, profound.

Each crystal formed a tale to tell,
Of journeys taken through winter's spell,
The dance of shadows, the flicker of hope,
In this cold world, we learn to cope.

Night falls softly, cloaking all,
Wrapping existence in its thrall,
Yet in the dark, a warmth persists,
Crystalline echoes of blissful trysts.

As dawn approaches, the cycle starts,
A vivid reminder within our hearts,
That even in darkness, we shall find,
The crystalline beauty that life designed.

Faint Impressions on the Icy Surface

Footprints linger on the frost,
Imprints left but never lost.
Glimmers dance in morning light,
A silent trace, a ghostly sight.

Nature holds its breath so still,
Crystals gleam on every hill.
Whispers soft beneath the sheen,
Memories of what once has been.

Winds caress the frozen ground,
In their touch, lost dreams are found.
Every breath a fleeting sign,
Faint impressions, yours and mine.

Through the haze of winter's grace,
Weaves a tale time can't erase.
Reflections on the icy sea,
Each moment, a memory.

Beneath the surface, stories flow,
Silent secrets kept below.
In the chill, we find our way,
Faint impressions lead the day.

Luminous Shadows of the Snowfall

Snowflakes whisper on the breeze,
Painting earth with gentle ease.
Luminous under evening's glow,
Dancing softly, ebb and flow.

Shadows stretch across the night,
Mysterious, soft and white.
A tranquil world, adorned in lace,
In this calm, we find our place.

Moonlight waltzes on the ground,
Silent music all around.
Every flake a shimmering dream,
Caught in winter's silver beam.

As the quiet settles deep,
Secrets of the night we keep.
Luminous shadows guide our way,
Through the stillness, hearts will sway.

In this moment, time stands still,
Nature's heart, a gentle thrill.
Beneath the stars, we will fall,
Into the snow's enchanting call.

Haunting Patterns in Winter’s Embrace

Snow drapes low on boughs of pine,
Whispers echo, soft and fine.
In patterns carved by winter's hand,
Memories rest in this stark land.

Footsteps silent, hearts entwined,
In this hush, our souls aligned.
Ghostly traces sketch the ground,
In every shadow, love is found.

The chill bites, but warmth remains,
In the heart, where joy sustains.
Haunting patterns weave a tale,
Of winters past that still prevail.

Beneath the frost, the world sleeps tight,
Covered in a quilt of white.
Stories unfold with every breeze,
In winter’s arms, we find our ease.

Each breath lingers in the air,
As we share what’s truly rare.
In patterns of frost, we remain,
Entwined forever in winter's chain.

Whispers Beneath the Snowy Canopy

Beneath the trees, where snowflakes fall,
Nature's voice, a gentle call.
Whispers soft on frozen ground,
In the silence, peace is found.

Branches bow with icy weight,
Holding secrets that await.
In the hush, the world retreats,
Each heartbeat, a rhythm repeats.

Footprints fade in the soft white,
Echoes lost in the still night.
Whispers weave through the chilly air,
Tales of wonder, light as prayer.

As twilight drapes a velvet cloak,
The world awakens, dreams evoke.
Beneath the canopy, we share,
Moments fleeting, light as air.

In every drift and gentle sigh,
The whispers of the earth nearby.
In winter’s hold, we find our way,
Beneath the snow, love's bright array.

The Secret Language of the Frost

In whispers cold, the frost will speak,
Each crystal sharp, a truth to seek.
It drafts a tale, in silence bold,
Of winter's heart, in icy hold.

Secrets wrapped in silver lace,
No voice to break their quiet grace.
Through windows clear, they weave and twine,
A hidden story, pure design.

Beneath the chill, old memories stir,
Nature's breath, a soft murmur.
From branches bare, to ground below,
The quiet words of frost do flow.

Life pauses here, in shimmer bright,
As day concedes to velvet night.
A language lost, yet crystal clear,
The secrets dwell, we hold them dear.

Each leaf a page, each flake a line,
In frost's embrace, the world aligns.
Listen close as winter sighs,
In its cold cradle, beauty lies.

Shadows Cast by the Bright Moon

The moonlight spills on silent ground,
Where shadows dance, where dreams are found.
It paints the night with silver gleam,
In whispered tones, we start to dream.

Glistening paths through darkened air,
Each shadow holds a hidden prayer.
They twist and turn, in playful chase,
As night embraces their fleeting grace.

Under the gaze of watchful stars,
The world unfolds, revealing scars.
In moonlit glow, our fears take flight,
Illuminating wrongs to right.

In every corner, stories hide,
Beneath the moon, they gently bide.
With every sigh, the shadows grow,
A secret song, they softly show.

A fleeting image, a moment’s glance,
In twilight's hold, shadows dance.
And as we walk, our hearts will yearn,
For the night’s embrace, our dreams return.

Allure of the Icy Mirage

A distant shimmer, bright and clear,
The icy mirage draws us near.
It dances lightly on the breeze,
A fleeting glimpse, a tease with ease.

Through frosted glass, the world confined,
A charm that captivates the blind.
We chase the light, a spectral game,
Each fleeting moment, never the same.

Within the chill, a beauty lies,
A tapestry of frozen skies.
Yet as we reach, it slips away,
A whisper lost, at break of day.

With every step, the vision fades,
In memory’s depths, a heart invades.
We linger long in winter's dream,
Caught in the threads of a shining seam.

The allure calls, though never real,
A phantom touch, a frost-kissed feel.
As twilight softens, shadows grow,
The icy mirage, a tale of woe.

Traces of Misfits in the Snow

In the soft hush of fallen snow,
Traces linger, whispers slow.
Footsteps zigzag, a dance of chance,
Echoing tales in winter's glance.

Each footprint tells of journeys made,
Of wanderers lost in twilight's shade.
The misfits roam, their spirits free,
In snowy realms, where dreams can be.

With hearts unbound, they chase the light,
Through frosty woods, in starry night.
Leaving behind the path they tread,
In every flake, a story led.

As snowflakes swirl, they weave and flow,
The tales of those who dared to go.
Amongst the white, their laughter rings,
A testament to life's wild swings.

In every drift, the echoes stay,
Of misfit souls who found their way.
In winter's grasp, a truth so pure,
Their traces linger, hearts endure.

Veils of Snow and Secrets Told

In the hush of night’s embrace,
Snowflakes dance, a whispered grace.
Veils of white, soft and pure,
Secrets held in silence lure.

Footsteps trap the fleeting dreams,
As the world unfolds in seams.
Underneath the moon's soft glow,
Fractals weave the tales of snow.

Beneath the branches, shadows play,
Softly drifting far away.
In the deep, untouched expanse,
Each drift whispers a secret dance.

Old memories in frosted air,
Winds of time, a gentle care.
Lost and found in winter's breath,
Life is born from winter’s depth.

Hazy Figures in Frosted Air

Figures emerge in morning haze,
Frosted breath, a ghostly maze.
Stirring softly, they ignite,
Shadows swirling in the light.

Curtains drawn in pale refrains,
Fluttering like forgotten chains.
Echoes whisper secrets far,
Traces left beneath the star.

Through the mist, their presence glows,
Wandering where the stillness flows.
Hints of laughter, sighs of woe,
In the dance of the frost they know.

Time suspended, shadows tease,
In the quiet, they find ease.
Caught between the worlds we see,
Frosted air, a memory.

The Quiet Remnants of Light

When evening falls, the remnants glow,
Softly fading, a gentle show.
In hidden corners, whispers dwell,
Telling tales that time won't quell.

The twilight wraps the world in grace,
Each flicker finds its rightful place.
Stars emerge with secret might,
Painting dreams in the dark of night.

Reflections shimmer on the lake,
Mirroring the night's sweet ache.
A soft embrace of dusk's soft sigh,
Where the remnants of light quietly lie.

In the stillness, hearts align,
Awakening the dream divine.
As shadows dance in soft delight,
We find peace in the quiet light.

Ghostly Figures Under the Stars

Beneath the sky, a canvas wide,
Ghostly figures' silent stride.
Starlight glimmers in their eyes,
As they weave through midnight skies.

Echoes of a distant past,
In the firmament, shadows cast.
Hand in hand, they sway and twirl,
In the stillness, time unfurls.

Whispers travel on the breeze,
Filling hearts with tender ease.
Veiled in mist, they softly tread,
Entwined with dreams where spirits led.

Each movement tells a hidden tale,
Of love that sails beyond the veil.
In the night, they take their flight,
Ghostly figures under the stars' light.

Phantom Shapes in the Cold Light

Whispers dance in shadows low,
Glimmers flicker, ebb and flow.
In the frost, they softly glide,
Phantoms play where secrets hide.

Veils of mist, they weave and spin,
Echoes murmur from within.
In the stillness, dreams take flight,
Phantom shapes in cold moonlight.

Figures shift on winter's breath,
Silent signs of life and death.
Midnight's chill embraces all,
Phantom shades in twilight's thrall.

Footfalls trace through the silent snow,
Fading faint, then start to grow.
Illusions born of frost and chill,
Haunting hearts, the night stands still.

Lurking Beneath the Powder

Beneath the crust, old stories sleep,
Ghosts of winter, dark and deep.
Layered whispers, time confined,
Lurking shapes that tease the mind.

Shadows sweep the jeweled ground,
Silent secrets barely found.
Crystals form a frozen shell,
Lurking echoes weave a spell.

Brittle branches, bent with weight,
Nature's breath, a lingering fate.
In the cold, a hidden fire,
Lurking thoughts that never tire.

Tales of frost entwined with dusk,
Fragrant air, sweet yet brusque.
In the stillness, pulses thrum,
Lurking spirits softly come.

Silhouettes Against a Frozen Sky

Dark against the shimm'ring white,
Silhouettes emerge at night.
Branches claw the starry dome,
Figures dance, no place like home.

Frosted breaths upon the glass,
Whispers pass as moments pass.
Ghostly forms with secrets sewn,
Silhouettes in pale moon's throne.

Beneath the vast and frozen sea,
Waves of stillness, wild and free.
Every shadow tells a tale,
Silhouettes that never pale.

In the calm, a world unfolds,
Nature's grip, both warm and cold.
Painted skies where dreams reside,
Silhouettes with time as guide.

Glistening Forms in the Chill

Twinkles form in icy breath,
Life and light defy the death.
Frozen diamonds, bright and clear,
Glistening forms, they draw us near.

Crisp and bright, the edges gleam,
Nature weaves a winning dream.
In this realm of frost and fire,
Glistening shapes that never tire.

Chill of night, a tender kind,
Messes with the heart and mind.
Within the freeze, hope finds its call,
Glistening dreams that bind us all.

So let the cold embrace your skin,
In frozen realms, the warmth begins.
Crafted magic, pure and still,
Glistening forms against the chill.

Veils of Frosted Darkness

In the night, shadows creep,
Veils of frost from silence steep.
Whispers of winter's chill breath,
Wrap the world in a shroud of death.

Moonlight dances, pale and thin,
Over the snow, where dreams begin.
A shiver runs through the air,
As secrets hide in darkness, rare.

Branches bend with crystal weight,
Marking time, weaving fate.
Lost in the clutch of endless night,
Veils of darkness hide the light.

Beyond the veil, a soft glow glints,
A flicker of hope, where heart still hints.
In the frost, life waits to sway,
Time shall break the darkness' play.

When dawn breaks, the frost shall fade,
And in the light, dreams unmade.
But in the shadows, whispers stay,
Veils of frost will always play.

Murmurs Beneath a Shimmering Sheet

Silent night, a blanket spread,
Whispers dance in silver thread.
Crystals formed in twilight's grace,
Glisten softly, nature's lace.

Beneath the shine, a world concealed,
Murmurs of love, promises revealed.
Every flake a story to share,
In harmony, twirling through the air.

Promises made in the still of night,
Carried on winds that hold them tight.
Underneath this shimmering sheet,
Life's heartbeat whispers, bittersweet.

Where shadows lie, and secrets breathe,
Murmurs drift from each soft wreath.
Winter's cloak, a tranquil sound,
In its fold, life's threads abound.

As the dawn tiptoes, so serene,
The murmurs fade, yet still they glean.
Memories held in the hush of snow,
Beneath the shimmering sheet, they flow.

Glimmers of Dusk in the Drifts

In twilight's arms, the day departs,
Glimmers of dusk warm hidden hearts.
Snowflakes twirl in a wistful dance,
Capturing dreams in a fleeting glance.

Softly they fall, a gentle grace,
Painting the world in a muted lace.
Each drift a promise, time unfolds,
Memories wrapped in the night's cold holds.

Breath of twilight, tender and light,
Guiding the stars to spark the night.
In the hush, where silence beams,
Whispers of hope are born from dreams.

Fading hues of the evening sky,
Where shadows linger and memories lie.
Glimmers break through, like fireflies' gleam,
In the drifts, we find our dream.

As night embraces every sigh,
Glimmers lead us by and by.
In winter's fold, life breathes anew,
Dusk's gentle kiss, a promise true.

Haunting Forms Beneath the Flurries

In the stillness, shadows form,
Haunting figures in the storm.
Flurries weave a ghostly dance,
Through the night, they take their chance.

Whispers echo in the gale,
Stories of souls that weave and sail.
Each flake a memory, soft and bright,
A fleeting moment lost to night.

Lurking shapes in the swirling white,
Reaching out for lost delight.
Haunting dreams in the winter's clutch,
A silent chill, a gentle touch.

Beneath the snow, the past remains,
Ghostly laughter, silent pains.
Forms that drift in spectral light,
Marking time through endless night.

As dawn breaks, the phantoms sway,
Fading slowly with the day.
Yet in the depths where flurries lie,
Haunting forms shall never die.

Wraiths Among the Frozen Pines

In shadows deep, the wraiths do weave,
Among the pines where none believe.
A whisper cold, their haunting song,
Echoes where the lost belong.

Frosted branches sway and bend,
As time slips past, a silent friend.
In each soft flake, a story hides,
Of faded trails and longing tides.

Their forms are shrouded, pale and light,
Against the dark, they dance in flight.
Entwined with mist and snow so pure,
They linger still, forever sure.

Through frozen breaths and chilling air,
The wraiths entwine without a care.
In the whispered sighs of winter's night,
They find their place, just out of sight.

Among the pines, they softly trace,
The memories of a forgotten face.
In twilight's grip, their stories spun,
Wraiths among the frozen, gathered as one.

The Forgotten Fragments of Twilight

In twilight's hush, where shadows creep,
Forgotten fragments stir from sleep.
A whisper of lost days and nights,
Capturing dreams in fading lights.

The world wears a veil of soft despair,
As echoes linger in the air.
Skeletal trees reach high above,
Cradling secrets of buried love.

Dim stars blink through a misty shroud,
Bearing witness to the dreaming crowd.
From bridges built on hopes now gone,
Shifting figures dance until dawn.

In the embrace of the muted glow,
The past etches tales too deep to show.
Fragments scatter like fallen leaves,
Whispering truths that the twilight weaves.

Yet hope remains in the fading light,
Where shadows stir into the night.
In the chill, their shapes dissolve,
As memories pulse, seeking to evolve.

Mirage of the Icy Fable

In the heart of winter's breath,
An icy fable dances with death.
Mirages shimmer, beguiled in grace,
While whispers weave through time and space.

Crystal forms and spectral light,
Twist and twine in the hushed night.
Each breath a tale of frost and chill,
Where time stands still, the air is still.

Figures flicker on the edge of sight,
Crafted from shadows, flickering bright.
With each step into the frozen glade,
The line between worlds begins to fade.

A mirror speaks in icy tones,
Reflecting dreams that chill to bones.
In this mirage, where silence reigns,
The fables of winter whisper their pains.

Yet amidst the cold, a fire glows,
A warmth that thrives where the wild wind blows.
In every breath of the icy air,
The fables live on, a tale to share.

Ephemeral Figures in the Cold

In the quiet chill of the evening glow,
Ephemeral figures drift, soft and slow.
Tracing patterns on the frozen ground,
Echoes of laughter in silence found.

With every gust, they seem to sway,
Fleeting shadows at the end of day.
The frost bites deep, yet they remain,
A dance of whispers, a haunting refrain.

Once vibrant lives, now cloaked in ice,
Their laughter lingers, a sweet sacrifice.
Among the trees, their stories blend,
In visions frozen, where echoes mend.

Through the frost, they weave and twirl,
In an eternal night, their spirits swirl.
With delicate grace, they fade away,
Leaving behind the warmth of play.

In the stillness, they softly sigh,
As the moon watches from the sky.
Ephemeral figures, lost in the cold,
Beacons of memory, whispered and bold.

Beckoning Forms Beneath Snowflakes

Amidst the quiet earth, they lie,
Figures drift softly, whispering shy.
Snowflakes gather, a gentle embrace,
Forming shadows in their traced space.

Each flake a story, a moment confined,
Carving memories, as past intertwines.
Beneath the white veil, secrets remain,
Awakening dreams wrapped in winter’s chain.

The branches bow low, each laden with weight,
Carving silhouettes of a delicate fate.
In the stillness, the world holds its breath,
Embracing the peace found in nature's depth.

But as sunlight warms, the forms start to fade,
The whispers of winter, a gentle charade.
In melting silence, they shift into air,
Beckoning us to remember, to care.

So linger a moment, let shadows remain,
In the dance of the snow, there's beauty in pain.
For beneath the white shroud, life starts anew,
In beckoning forms, we find what is true.

Wisps of Darkness in the Frosty Air

Whispers of night swirl in the blue,
Adrift on the breeze, tales old yet new.
Darkness embraces, a shiver ignites,
Through frosty storefronts and shadowy nights.

In the heart of the chill, there's magic untold,
As wisps shape the silence, forming bold.
Each corner hides echoes of laughter and cries,
As the moon pours its silver from starlit skies.

Footsteps are muffled, soft secrets unfold,
As frost paints the windows, a story retold.
The chill in the air, an ethereal bite,
Wraps hearts in reflections of sweet, haunting light.

Yet in the depths of the stillness we find,
A warmth that can pierce through the frost and the blind.
For love holds its fire, igniting the cold,
While wisps of darkness weave threads of pure gold.

In every breath taken, the echoes remain,
Of kindness and hope mingled within pain.
So when the shadows come, do not despair,
For there’s light in the wisps that sweep through the air.

Undercurrents of a Winter's Dream

Beneath the surface, the rivers still flow,
In winter's embrace, where secrets bestow.
Currents whisper softly, beneath the ice,
Treading paths of dreams, both gentle and nice.

The world upon frost, so tranquil and white,
But linger just long, and you'll sense the slight.
Life courses beneath, in hidden refrain,
While colors lie dormant, waiting for rain.

A soft sigh emerges, from depths far and wide,
As snowflakes descend, on the waters they glide.
Each flake is a promise, a dream to behold,
In the hush of the night, stories unfold.

With every heartbeat, time slips through our hands,
As winter holds blessings, in crystalline strands.
So listen with care, to the currents that call,
For in winter's embrace, we're alive in it all.

The undercurrents churn, deep in their flight,
Painting vibrance in shadows, beneath pale moonlight.
So dream in the winter, as white drapes the night,
Embrace all the mysteries, hold them tight.

The Melancholy of Covered Paths

Through paths that are hidden, snow softly falls,
Each step heavy-laden, the silence enthralls.
The trees stand like sentinels, tall and bare,
Guarding the secrets of the world laid bare.

Covered in white, the footprints erased,
Memories linger, but time has displaced.
Echoes of laughter, now whispers of woe,
In the melancholy that blankets below.

The air thick with longing, yet crisp with the chill,
It weaves through the branches, a silence so still.
Each breath is a sigh, drawn from the heart's well,
As shadows dance softly, invoking farewell.

But though the paths murmur of pain and of loss,
Within those folds lie the seeds we emboss.
For even in winter, where sorrows combine,
Spring waits in the wings, with beauty divine.

The paths may be covered, but hope still remains,
Line by line's sketching the history's stains.
So wander with care through the snow-laden way,
For within every step, life'll find a way.

Dappled Lights Upon Winter's Canvas

In twilight's grip, the shadows play,
Dappled lights in the fading day.
The snowflakes dance, all spirits soar,
Upon winter's canvas, we explore.

Whispers of warmth in the chilly air,
Nature's magic, beyond compare.
Each twinkle brightens the muted hue,
In this frozen world, dreams come true.

Trees stand tall, their limbs adorned,
In sparkling crowns, the night is warmed.
Every snowdrift a story tells,
Of quiet nights and secret spells.

Footprints crunch on the pristine ground,
Echoes linger, a soft, sweet sound.
Under the stars, our spirits meet,
In dappled lights, our hearts skip a beat.

With every breath, the world unfolds,
Winter's magic, a sight to behold.
As nature sleeps, our hearts ignite,
In dappled lights, we find our light.

Chilling Spirits Beneath a Silver Glow

Beneath the moon, the shadows creep,
Chilling spirits in silence sweep.
The silver glow, a haunting sight,
In this stillness of winter's night.

Whispers low in the frosty breeze,
Gentle moments, a soft unease.
Every glance holds a hidden tale,
Of wandering souls, a ghostly trail.

Branches shiver, the air runs cold,
Magic lingers, the night unfolds.
With every sigh, the world holds breath,
In chilling spirits, we dance with death.

Stars above glitter, faint and far,
Guide us softly, like a distant star.
In this realm where shadows flow,
We embrace the chill beneath the glow.

As time drips slow like melting ice,
The heart finds warmth, a hidden spice.
Chilling spirits, we welcome here,
In the silver glow, we lose our fear.

Faded Whispers in the Frost

Morning breaks with a frosted kiss,
Faded whispers in winter's bliss.
Silence drapes the slumbering ground,
In the stillness, peace is found.

Leaves of yesterday, crisp and brown,
Lie gently wrapped in winter's gown.
Each breath a cloud in the cold air,
Faded memories linger there.

Curled beneath blankets, warmth we crave,
In the frost, old dreams we save.
Embers of laughter, soft and shy,
Dance like shadows against the sky.

With every step, the crunching sound,
Unveils the magic all around.
Faded whispers echo and sigh,
In the frosty world, they will fly.

As night descends, the pale moon beams,
Igniting again our winter dreams.
In the silence, our hearts can boast,
Of faded whispers we love the most.

Glistening Shadows Beneath the Stars

Under a blanket of shimmering night,
Glistening shadows in soft moonlight.
Stars above, like diamonds bright,
Guide our paths with their tender light.

A whispering wind stirs dreams anew,
As twinkling tails paint the deep blue.
Each glimmer beckons with a gentle call,
In the stillness, we find our all.

Footsteps soft on the frozen ground,
Echoes of laughter surround.
In this dance, our hearts entwine,
Beneath the stars, your hand in mine.

The world fades into a gentle haze,
As we follow the glow of the starry maze.
In glistening shadows, we twirl and spin,
In this moment, our souls begin.

As dawn approaches, the night will yield,
But in memories, our hearts are sealed.
Glistening shadows forever remain,
Beneath the stars, we'll meet again.

Faint Traces of the Wandering Star

In the velvet sky, whispers roam,
Faint traces left, they call me home.
A fleeting glow, a soft embrace,
Guiding my heart through endless space.

Among the clouds, shadows dance,
Flickering lights in a cosmic trance.
Each twinkle tells stories of old,
Of journeys taken, of dreams untold.

As twilight fades, the night unfurls,
The star's soft presence softly swirls.
In stillness deep, I feel it near,
A gentle echo, a voice sincere.

Chasing trails of the bright unknown,
In whispered secrets, I'm never alone.
A charted path of the skies above,
Illuminated by the light of love.

Through time and space, I seek and find,
The lingering light that guides the blind.
Faint traces linger, a promise kept,
In the heart of night, my spirit leapt.

Illusions of Light in the Quiet

Silence drapes like a velvet shawl,
Illusions shimmer, then start to fall.
Between the whispers, shadows play,
In the quiet dusk, the night holds sway.

Flickers of gold in a sea of gray,
Hopes intertwined, they lead astray.
Glimmers of laughter in a serene hush,
A symphony formed in the gentle blush.

The ambient glow of softened dreams,
Weaving through stray, ethereal beams.
Each pulse of light, a fleeting thrill,
In the void of night, time stands still.

Captured moments, they rise and fall,
In the echoes of night, I hear their call.
Whispers of joy in shadowed flight,
Crafting illusions that dance with light.

As dawn approaches, these dreams may fade,
Yet the echoes linger, never betrayed.
In the quietude, I find my way,
Illusions of light, forever they play.

Traces of an Unseen Dance

In the silent dusk, movements sneak,
Traces of rhythm, soft and meek.
Echoes of grace that drift and sway,
In the shadows, they find their way.

Whispered steps on a moonlit floor,
Each turn reveals what came before.
An unseen dance in the night's embrace,
Time spins gently, a fleeting trace.

Underneath stars, the magic flows,
Where ebbing tides of the heart compose.
A melody born in the space between,
Where all is felt, yet nothing's seen.

Softly they twirl in a twilight haze,
Unraveling secrets in subtle plays.
Each breath a note in the evening's song,
Telling a tale where we both belong.

As shadows merge and starlight wanes,
The dance continues, its essence remains.
In the quiet night, we hear our chance,
Embracing the beauty of our trance.

Frosted Reflections of Hidden Paths

Under a blanket of twinkling frost,
Rest the secrets of time long lost.
Nature's whispers in the crisp, cold air,
Guide our steps with a tender care.

Mirrored whispers on the frozen ground,
Frosted reflections in silence found.
Each path we tread paints stories clear,
In the still of winter, we draw near.

Beneath the glimmers of icy lace,
Hidden paths weave in a silent space.
Footprints linger, a silent guide,
Leading the way where the heart resides.

As shadows lengthen and daylight fades,
The frosted world in twilight parades.
Paths intertwine, a gentle embrace,
In the stillness, we find our place.

Voices carried on the chilly breeze,
Echo the dreams beneath the trees.
Frosted reflections will always stay,
Guiding us home, come what may.

Enigmatic Forms in the Winter Hush

In shadows deep, the silence sweeps,
A cloak of white where stillness keeps.
Shapes emerge in frostbit air,
Nature's art laid bare.

Whispers ride on icy breeze,
Mysteries hide among the trees.
Footprints trace the quiet ground,
Where lost and found intertwine around.

Bitter cold, yet warmly spun,
In the hush, all things are one.
Fleeting moments slip away,
In winter's grasp, they softly lay.

Glimmers shine on silent nights,
Underneath the stars' soft lights.
Echoes dance in moonlit beams,
In the stillness, hope redeems.

An enigmatic world unfolds,
In each flake, a story told.
Boundless beauty, quiet grace,
In winter's arms, we find our place.

The Winter’s Silent Specter

The world is hushed, a breath held tight,
As winter weaves her cloak of white.
Trees stand tall, arms raised to God,
In reverence, they stand awed.

A specter roams this frozen land,
With gentle touch and careful hand.
Shimmering crystals catch the eye,
As whispers of the past drift by.

Each step taken on the snow,
Reveals adventures lost in woe.
A ballet of shadows, soft and slow,
In the quiet, a tale starts to grow.

All is still, yet life abounds,
In the silence, the heart resounds.
Veils of frost, a mystic veil,
In winter's grasp, no tale is pale.

The specter fades at break of dawn,
Leaving traces, but soon is gone.
A promise made, a hope held near,
In winter's heart, we persevere.

Ethereal Prints in the Powdered White

In powdered white, the earth is dressed,
With ethereal prints, the world at rest.
A canvas fresh, where stories start,
Each mark a whisper from the heart.

Softly fallen, flakes descend,
A gentle touch, as if to mend.
They cover all with tender grace,
Creating magic in every space.

Footsteps echo on this stage,
In winter's book, we turn the page.
Each imprint speaks, a tale untold,
In the frostbit air, memories fold.

From quiet woods to open fields,
Nature's charm, a winter's shield.
Ethereal forms in the fading light,
Guide the soul through the enchanted night.

With each dawn, the beauty fades,
But in our hearts, the memory wades.
Frozen dreams in white expanse,
In fleeting grace, we find our dance.

A Luminous Drift of Lost Voices

A luminous drift of voices lost,
In the silence of winter, we count the cost.
Echoes linger in frosty air,
A chorus of dreams, a silent prayer.

Snowflakes whisper tales of old,
Each one unique, each one bold.
They shimmer softly in twilight's glow,
As stories weave through the flakes that flow.

Footsteps vanish beneath the white,
As echoes fade into the night.
A memory bound in the soft embrace,
Of winter’s chill, a sacred space.

Luminous threads of lost desire,
Dance like flames in a fading fire.
They wrap around the heart anew,
In the cold, they find their view.

With every breath, the past ignites,
Painting shadows in the twilight lights.
A drift of voices, soft and clear,
In winter's arms, we hold them near.

Beneath the Surface of White Stillness

In the quiet of winter's embrace,
Silence whispers, a gentle trace.
Snowflakes dance in soft twilight,
Beneath the surface, dreams take flight.

Frozen streams hold secrets tight,
Beneath the ice, a hidden sight.
Echoes of life in shadows creep,
While the world is lulled to sleep.

Footprints imprint the snow's white skin,
Stories of where we've been, begin.
Nature's stillness speaks in hearts,
Crafting tales as winter departs.

Branches sway, adorned with gems,
Icicles hang like nature's hems.
Beneath the surface lies the spark,
Of vibrant life, igniting the dark.

Whispers of warmth, a promise made,
As the winter's chill starts to fade.
Beneath the surface, hope resides,
In the stillness, love abides.

Flights of Fancy in Frosted Hues

In the dawn of frosted light,
Dreams take wing, in pure delight.
Colors dance on icy streams,
Painting winter's whispered dreams.

With every breath, a story we weave,
In the frost, our hearts believe.
Sparkling crystals, shimmer and glow,
In the magic of winter's show.

Clouds drift by in delicate veil,
Carrying whispers of each tale.
With a heart unfettered and free,
Flights of fancy beckon thee.

The world transforms, a canvas bright,
Each hue a brushstroke, pure delight.
We dance among the frozen dreams,
In awe of nature's radiant schemes.

Let us chase the fleeting light,
Through the hush of the starry night.
In frosted hues, our spirits soar,
A journey beckoning evermore.

Ghostly Shapes on a Wintry Canvas

Shadows linger, soft and pale,
Ghostly shapes in snow's white veil.
Figures flit through frosty air,
A haunting waltz, the world laid bare.

Footprints vanish, whispers call,
Echoes of laughter, a soft sprawl.
Nature’s breath, a silent sight,
Ghostly shapes in winter's night.

Veils of mist swirl in the trees,
Carrying secrets upon the breeze.
With each gust, a tale unfolds,
Of ancient dreams and futures bold.

Moonlight dances upon the snow,
Sketching figures, fast and slow.
In the twilight, visions gleam,
Ghostly shapes within a dream.

Breathe in the chill, let spirits roam,
In frozen fields, we find our home.
For in the night, we lose and find,
The ghostly shapes that bind mankind.

Eclipsed by Ice and Snow

The sun dips low, the light grows dim,
As shadows stretch, on winter's whim.
Eclipsed by ice, the world awaits,
Silent wonders behind the gates.

Snowflakes gather, blanket white,
Hiding stories deep from sight.
Each crystal glimmers, cold and bright,
In the stillness, day turns night.

Nature's breath, a frozen sigh,
Underneath the vast, dark sky.
Whispers of warmth, elusive, shy,
Echo in the cold, nigh.

Trees stand tall, adorned in grace,
Guardians of this tranquil space.
Eclipsed by ice, yet steadfast still,
In the chill, dreams start to thrill.

As winter wanes, the light returns,
Hope ignites, and quietly churns.
Eclipsed no more, the thaw begins,
Life unfurls, in vibrant spins.

Veils of Silence in the Cold

In the hush of winter's breath,
Whispers dance like shadows,
Blankets of snow lay in rest,
Covering all that follows.

Branches bend beneath the weight,
Silence wraps the sleeping earth,
Veils of frost at every gate,
Nature's calm, a tender mirth.

Stars emerge in velvet skies,
Glimmers soft on frozen streams,
Echoes fade, as if to sigh,
Hidden truths in muted dreams.

Footprints barely leave a trace,
Windswept paths of whispered thought,
In the stillness, find your place,
In this world where time is caught.

Night will yield to morning's light,
Yet the silence, still remains,
Veils of cold in tranquil sight,
Guarding secrets, holding pains.

Chasing Nocturnal Dreams

Beneath the moon's soft, silver glow,
Dreams take flight on whispered winds,
Through the night, we chase the flow,
Where reality bends and spins.

Stars twinkle like distant hearts,
Illuminating paths unknown,
In the dark, a story starts,
With every thought that's ever grown.

Winds of night, they softly call,
Guiding us through shadow's sway,
In this dance, we risk the fall,
Embracing night's enchanting play.

Echoes linger in the dawn,
Fleeting moments fade from sight,
Yet the dreams not truly gone,
In our hearts, they burn so bright.

Chasing visions lost in time,
Where hopes and fears intertwine,
With each pulse, we reach, we climb,
Innocent in night's design.

Footfalls in a Dappled Glow

Amidst the woods where shadows weave,
Footfalls wander, soft and light,
Dappled sun through leafy eaves,
Whispers beckon, heart takes flight.

Paths of gold beneath our feet,
Swaying branches hum a tune,
Nature's rhythm, fresh and sweet,
Guiding us from noon to moon.

Every step, a story told,
In the rustle, life unfolds,
Moments caught in beams of gold,
As the forest softly molds.

Mossy banks and gentle streams,
Crickets sing their evening song,
In this realm of waking dreams,
We belong, where hearts are strong.

As daylight fades, the glow remains,
Carried softly on the breeze,
In the woods, our joy sustains,
Lost in time, we find our peace.

Gleams of Frost’s Embrace

Morning breaks on a world of glass,
Frosty whispers kiss the dawn,
Each breath fogged, the moments pass,
Nature’s art on lawns is drawn.

Gems of ice on tangled vines,
Nature’s brush in frozen grace,
Every sparkle, purpose shines,
Cloaked in winter’s soft embrace.

Sunrise paints the landscape bright,
Casting shadows long and pale,
In the stillness, pure delight,
Caught in winter's whispered tale.

With each sunbeam, secrets thaw,
Petals bloom as light draws near,
Life awakens, free from draw,
In this season’s fleeting cheer.

Gleams of frost, a fleeting rhyme,
Moments cherished, quickly fade,
In the dance of space and time,
Nature's beauty, serenade.

Whispers of Winter's Veil

Silent whispers in the breeze,
Softly carried through the trees.
Snowflakes dance on chilly air,
Winter's magic everywhere.

Crisp and clear, the world is still,
Blanketed by nature’s thrill.
Footsteps crunch on frosty ground,
In this peace, serenity found.

Bare branches sway with gentle grace,
Stars twinkle in the velvet space.
Moonlight drapes a silver sheet,
As night wraps the earth in retreat.

Icicles hang like diamond light,
Glistening softly in the night.
Winter's chill, a soothing balm,
In this quiet, there’s a calm.

Warmth of fireside, stories shared,
Embers glow as hearts are bared.
Whispers weave through cozy rooms,
In winter's veil, love blooms and blooms.

Frosted Echoes of the Night

Silent shadows softly creep,
Moonlight whispers, secrets keep.
Frosted air, a biting chill,
Nature sleeps, her dreams fulfill.

Stars above like diamonds shine,
In the dark, a world divine.
Echoes dance through dreamer's mind,
In the stillness, solace find.

Crisp the air, the night an art,
Winter's brush paints every part.
Footprints linger on the snow,
Guiding where the heart may go.

Gentle winds hum frosty tunes,
Beneath the watchful, gleaming moons.
Each breath visible in the dark,
A fleeting moment, a quiet spark.

Hushed, the night begins to fade,
As dawn unveils the light displayed.
Frosted echoes fade away,
Yet winter's magic longs to stay.

Silhouettes Beneath the Light

Underneath the moon's embrace,
Shadows dance, a fleeting trace.
Silhouettes in silver glow,
Beneath the night, a world below.

Figures sway in gentle grace,
Lost in time in this still space.
Whispers carried on the breeze,
Stories told among the trees.

Each moment fleeting, soft and shy,
Time a whisper as it flies.
Glimmers catch the eyes of stars,
Each a wish, each a scar.

Light cascades through branches bare,
A tapestry of dreams laid there.
Silhouettes hold secrets tight,
In the quiet of the night.

Hearts entwined in muted hues,
Finding solace in the blues.
Underneath the moon’s soft sight,
Life breathes deep, out of the night.

Echoes linger, hearts take flight,
In the magic of the night.
Beneath the stars, we come alive,
In silhouettes, our spirits thrive.

Ghostly Footprints on White Ground

Footprints ghost across the snow,
Tracing paths where wild winds blow.
Whispers linger in the cold,
Stories waiting to be told.

Blankets of white, a soft embrace,
Nature's canvas, a quiet space.
Ghostly figures etched in frost,
Moments captured, never lost.

With each step, a tale unfolds,
Of winter's breath and magic bold.
Under stars, a truth is found,
In the silence, echoes sound.

Secrets hidden, dreams take flight,
Beneath the cloak of winter's night.
Where shadows play and silence reigns,
Ghostly footprints leave their stains.

Whispers carried through the trees,
In the air, enchanting pleas.
The world slows; tomorrow waits,
In each footprint, memory creates.

Frosted ground, a timeless scene,
In the chill, life feels serene.
Ghostly footprints in the snow,
Mark the tales of life below.

www.ingramcontent.com/pod-product-compliance
Ingram Content Group UK Ltd.
Pitfield, Milton Keynes, MK11 3LW, UK
UKHW031941151224
452382UK00006B/196

9 789916 799246